End-of-Pilot Assessment of the U.S. Army's Consolidated Recruiting Program

BRUCE R. ORVIS, MICHAEL VASSEUR, JENNIE W. WENGER,
CHRISTOPHER E. MAERZLUFT, MICHAEL G. SHANLEY,
AVERY CALKINS

Prepared for the United States Army
Approved for public release; distribution unlimited

RAND ARROYO CENTER

For more information on this publication, visit **www.rand.org/t/RRA955-1**.

About RAND

The RAND Corporation is a research organization that develops solutions to public policy challenges to help make communities throughout the world safer and more secure, healthier and more prosperous. RAND is nonprofit, nonpartisan, and committed to the public interest. To learn more about RAND, visit www.rand.org.

Research Integrity

Our mission to help improve policy and decisionmaking through research and analysis is enabled through our core values of quality and objectivity and our unwavering commitment to the highest level of integrity and ethical behavior. To help ensure our research and analysis are rigorous, objective, and nonpartisan, we subject our research publications to a robust and exacting quality-assurance process; avoid both the appearance and reality of financial and other conflicts of interest through staff training, project screening, and a policy of mandatory disclosure; and pursue transparency in our research engagements through our commitment to the open publication of our research findings and recommendations, disclosure of the source of funding of published research, and policies to ensure intellectual independence. For more information, visit www.rand.org/about/principles.

RAND's publications do not necessarily reflect the opinions of its research clients and sponsors.

Published by the RAND Corporation, Santa Monica, Calif.
© 2022 RAND Corporation
RAND® is a registered trademark.

Library of Congress Cataloging-in-Publication Data is available for this publication.
ISBN: 978-1-9774-0891-4

About This Report

This report documents research and analysis conducted as part of a project entitled *Consolidated Recruiting Pilot Program Evaluation, Year Three*, sponsored by the Assistant Secretary of the Army, Manpower and Reserve Affairs. The purpose of this project was, in accordance with recommendation 38 of the National Commission on the Future of the Army and the National Defense Authorization Act of 2017, to work with the Army to maintain, evaluate, and report on the results of the Consolidated Recruiting Program through its third year.

This research was conducted within RAND Arroyo Center's Personnel, Training, and Health Program. RAND Arroyo Center, part of the RAND Corporation, is a federally funded research and development center (FFRDC) sponsored by the United States Army.

RAND operates under a "Federal-Wide Assurance" (FWA00003425) and complies with the *Code of Federal Regulations for the Protection of Human Subjects Under United States Law* (45 CFR 46), also known as "the Common Rule," as well as with the implementation guidance set forth in DoD Instruction 3216.02. As applicable, this compliance includes reviews and approvals by RAND's Institutional Review Board (the Human Subjects Protection Committee) and by the U.S. Army. The views of sources utilized in this study are solely their own and do not represent the official policy or position of DoD or the U.S. Government.

Acknowledgments

We wish to thank the many persons in the Office of the Assistant Secretary of the Army (Manpower and Reserve Affairs (ASA[M&RA]), Headquarters Department of the Army (HQDA) G-1, the Army Marketing and Research Group (AMRG), USAREC, and the National Guard Bureau (NGB) whom we worked with and who assisted us in launching and evaluating the pilot program, and the recruiters who participated in our focus groups. In particular, we want to express our gratitude to Linden St. Clair (OASA[M&RA]); John Jessup, Chris Jackson, and Erin Clark (then, AMRG), MAJ Matt Riley and

MAJ Christopher Brown (NGB); Rick Ayer and MAJ Jonathan Seiter (then, HQ USAREC); Jonathan Norton and James Jensen (HQ USAREC); and COL Joanne Moore and COL Brian Basset (both then office of the ASA [M&RA] and HQDA G-1). We also would like to thank Paul Aswell (formerly Chief, Accessions Policy, Deputy Chief of Staff for Personnel, G-1), Jason Ward (RAND), and Shannon Desrosiers (Center for Naval Analyses) for their thoughtful reviews of this report and helpful suggestions. At RAND, we are grateful to all the programmers who assisted us: Jonas Kempf, Lisa Kraus, Judith Mele, and Christine DeMartini.

Summary

The Fiscal Year (FY) 2017 National Defense Authorization Act (NDAA) (Pub. L. 114-328, 2016) mandated a pilot test of a program in which Army recruiters were authorized to recruit individuals into any of the three components and to receive credit for an enlistee for a period of not less than three years. In June 2020, the test reached the three-year point since the first pilot site initiated operations under this Consolidated Recruiting Program (CRP).

This report provides the following: a three-year analysis of the effects that consolidated recruiting efforts had on the ability of recruiters to attract and place qualified candidates; a determination of the extent to which consolidating recruiting efforts affected efficiency; and a discussion of challenges associated with a recruiter working to recruit individuals to enlist in a component in which the recruiter may not have served and of the satisfaction of recruiters with the pilot program.

There are many differences across recruiting sites that likely influence the number and quality of recruits. Therefore, working with U.S. Army Recruiting Command (USAREC) and the Army National Guard (ARNG), we first established a framework that allowed for comparison across sites by selecting a series of balanced USAREC–ARNG test and comparison site pairs.

For these test and comparison sites, we assessed three measures of recruiters' ability to attract candidates: total enlistment contracts, high-quality contracts, and Army enlistment contracts as a percentage of all services' enlistment contracts written in a geographic area. We also assessed three metrics that may be tied to recruiting efficiency: the ratio of appointments made by recruiters to contracts produced, the Delayed Entry Program (DEP) attrition rates for cross-component recruits versus other recruits, and the attrition from reserve components (RC) units prior to training completion. Finally, we examined the number and characteristics of cross-component contracts relative to same component contracts.

Overall, the program's effects on contracts, market share, and efficiency were small and not statistically meaningful. Thus, we cannot conclude that the program had an effect on these outcomes. We did see differences between cross-component and same-component recruits: Cross-component recruits from USAREC into the ARNG received higher enlistment bonuses than recruits into the U.S. Army Reserve (USAR); this was driven by bonuses for recruits into combat positions, as well as those without Tier 1 education credentials and/or who did not score in Armed Forces Qualification Test Categories I–IIIA. All but two of the cross-component recruits from the ARNG to USAREC were recruited for active duty. Recruiters suggested that this was due to the recruit's desire to leave the geographic area or to secure a full-time job and related benefits. We also compared Military Occupational Specialty (MOS) area (i.e., combat, combat support, combat service support) between cross-component and same-component contracts but found no statistically meaningful difference. Similarly, when we compared DEP attrition between ARNG cross-component contracts into the Regular Army versus USAREC contracts for active duty, we found no meaningful difference. Finally, we compared completion of Initial Entry Training by 12–15 months after enlistment between USAREC cross-component contracts into the ARNG versus ARNG contracts into the ARNG; we found no statistically meaningful difference.

In addition to the statistical analysis, we conducted focus groups with recruiters at the test sites during the first two years of the program (FY 2018–FY 2019). Following the conclusion of the program, we also interviewed representatives at Headquarters, USAREC, obtained input from the National Guard Bureau, and conducted discussions with recruiters at the test sites that were most successful in writing cross-component contracts. The information we obtained provided insights into strengths and weaknesses of the CRP. Recruiters' experiences with the program were mixed: Some saw little value added and even an overall adverse effect on workload, while many at more-successful locations said that the program helped them make mission and lamented its termination. One difference between sites involved the relationship between the components in the test site pair. This relationship appeared to be better at the more successful sites; recruiters there noted several positive aspects of that communication and ways to further strengthen it, such as regular meetings of the local recruiters and managers for the two components to discuss emerging issues and resolve them.

Given the absence of statistically or substantively meaningful effects on contract production or recruiting efficiency, as well as certain stakeholder concerns, the Army decided to terminate the pilot program after the third year.

The weaknesses in the implementation of the program are highly likely to have contributed to the absence of meaningful differences in production between the test and comparison sites. While there may be potential for a consolidated recruiting program to strengthen Army recruiting, the specific motivational and operational impediments identified in our analysis of the pilot program would need to be overcome. Moreover, increasing the number of recruits enlisted into the Army would depend on how many potential recruits currently are lost due to limitations on writing cross-component contracts and on the number of available training seats and unit vacancies left to fill at any time. On balance, considering the organizational and operational changes required and related costs, the study team concluded that it is not likely that the Army can, particularly in the near term, overcome the challenges to launch a successful cross-component recruiting program.

Contents

APPENDIX

Tables

CHAPTER ONE

Introduction

The National Commission on the Future of the Army (NCFA) noted in its report that "the Army is intended to operate as one force—the Regular Army, Army National Guard, and the Army Reserve—[but that] gaps and seams exist in the Army's stated Total Force Policy." The Commission reported a "lack of recruiting unity of effort at the Army Headquarters and local levels." It noted that U.S. Army Recruiting Command (USAREC) is responsible for Regular Army (RA) and U.S. Army Reserve (USAR) recruiting, whereas each state is responsible for Army National Guard (ARNG) recruiting, and that "each component and state establishes its own recruiting goals." It further noted that, "At the local level, recruiters from each component vie for the dwindling population of potential recruits, possibly influencing an individual to join a component that may not be the best fit for that individual." The Commission concluded that, "Such unity of effort can achieve efficiencies and effectiveness while ensuring recruiting consistently produces the requisite quality and quantity of soldiers that all three components need." It therefore recommended that the Army establish a pilot program to better align recruiting efforts across the RA, ARNG, and USAR with the goal of ensuring that the Army is not effectively competing with itself for "a diminishing pool of qualified individuals." It further recommended that "Congress should authorize and direct the Secretary of the Army to establish a substantial multiyear pilot program in which recruiters from all three components are authorized to recruit individuals into any of the components and receive credit for an enlistee regardless of the component. Congress should specifically authorize the pilot program 'notwithstanding any other laws' in order to avoid potential fiscal law concerns" (NCFA, 2016, pp. 3, 72–73).

The Fiscal Year (FY) 2017 National Defense Authorization Act (NDAA; Pub. L. 114-328, 2016) mandated a pilot test for this program (the Consolidated Recruiting Program [CRP]) for a period of not less than three years. Specifically, Section 527 mandated the following:

"SEC. 527. CONSOLIDATION OF ARMY MARKETING AND PILOT PROGRAM ON CONSOLIDATED ARMY RECRUITING.

(a) CONSOLIDATION OF ARMY MARKETING.—Not later than October 1, 2017, the Secretary of the Army shall consolidate into a single organization within the Department of the Army all functions relating to the marketing of the Army and each of the components of the Army in order to assure unity of effort and cost effectiveness in the marketing of the Army and each of the components of the Army.

(b) PILOT PROGRAM ON CONSOLIDATED ARMY RECRUITING.—

(1) PILOT PROGRAM REQUIRED.—Not later than 180 days after the date of the enactment of this Act, the Secretary of the Army shall carry out a pilot program to consolidate the recruiting efforts of the Regular Army, Army Reserve, and Army National Guard under which a recruiter in one of the components participating in the pilot program may recruit individuals to enlist in any of the components regardless of the funding source of the recruiting activity.

(2) CREDIT TOWARD ENLISTMENT GOALS.— Under the pilot program, a recruiter shall receive credit toward periodic enlistment goals for each enlistment regardless of the component in which the individual enlists.

(3) DURATION.—The Secretary shall carry out the pilot program for a period of not less than three years.

(c) BRIEFING AND REPORTS.—

(1) BRIEFING ON CONSOLIDATION PLAN.—Not later than March 1, 2017, the Secretary of the Army shall provide to the Committees on Armed Services of the Senate and the House of Representatives a briefing on the Secretary's plan to carry out the Army marketing consolidation required by subsection (a).

(2) INTERIM REPORT ON PILOT PROGRAM.—

(A) IN GENERAL.—Not later than one year after the date on which the pilot program under subsection (b) commences, the Secretary shall submit to the congressional committees specified in paragraph (1) a report on the pilot program.

(B) ELEMENTS.—The report under subparagraph (A) shall include each of the following:

(i) An analysis of the effects that consolidated recruiting efforts has on the overall ability of recruiters to attract and place qualified candidates.

(ii) A determination of the extent to which consolidating recruiting efforts affects efficiency and recruiting costs.

(iii) An analysis of any challenges associated with a recruiter working to recruit individuals to enlist in a component in which the recruiter has not served.

(iv) An analysis of the satisfaction of recruiters and the component recruiting commands with the pilot program.

(3) FINAL REPORT ON PILOT PROGRAM.—Not later than 180 days after the date on which the pilot program is completed, the Secretary shall submit to the congressional committees specified in paragraph (1) a final report on the pilot program. The final report shall include any recommendations of the Secretary with respect to extending or making permanent the pilot program and a description of any related legislative actions

that the Secretary considers appropriate" (Pub. L. 114-328, 2016, pp. 2117–2118).

In June 2020, the test reached the three-year point since the first pilot site initiated operations under the program. (None of the other pilot sites initiated such operations until mid-January 2018.)

This report provides several analyses called out in section 527 of the FY 2017 NDAA, including the following: analysis of the effects that consolidating recruiting efforts had on recruiters' ability to attract and place qualified candidates; the extent to which consolidating recruiting efforts affected recruiting efficiency; challenges that recruiters reported in recruiting prospects into a component in which they had not served; and the satisfaction of recruiters and recruiting commands with the pilot program (Pub. L. 114-328, Section 527, 2016). The Army asked the RAND Corporation's Arroyo Center to conduct these analyses of the CRP; the study team provided ongoing support and analysis during the development, implementation, and assessment of the pilot program.

The remainder of this chapter begins with a discussion of selected literature on Army recruiting topics relevant to the pilot program. This section will discuss the reasons why a consolidated recruiting program might improve the Army's ability to attract and place high-quality candidates and improve recruiting efficiency, as well as the considerations required for successful implementation. The final section draws on this information to summarize the outcomes that we might expect from a consolidated recruiting program, before outlining the remaining chapters of this report.

Army Recruiting

Research on Army recruiting tends to focus on the supply of *high-quality* enlistment contracts, which are enlistment contracts for high school graduates with Armed Forces Qualification Test (AFQT) scores at or above the 50th percentile (the national average). High-quality contracts are supply-constrained because such individuals have relatively better prospects for civilian employment than non–high school graduates or those with lower AFQT scores. A number of different factors determine high-quality enlistment supply, including the strength of the economy, the use and management of recruiting resources—such as recruiters, advertising, bonuses, and education benefits—and youth interest in joining the Army and both of its reserve components (Asch, 2019, provides a review of the recent literature). The majority of the literature, especially the recent literature, has focused on recruiting for the active component, but older models of reserve recruiting suggest that the determinants of reserve enlisted supply are similar to the determinants of active-component enlisted supply, with the addition of the probability of mobilization and deployment (e.g., Arkes and Kilburn, 2005; Asch, 1993). A recent study also found similarity in the factors underlying enlisted supply in the active component and the Army Reserve (Orvis et al., forthcoming).

Recruiters and Incentives

Recruiters are an essential input to the supply of enlistment contracts. When executed properly, consolidating the recruiting process for USAREC and the ARNG should allow the three components to draw on a pool of shared recruiters that is larger than any of the components would otherwise have access to on its own without substantially increasing costs. Prior research suggests that expanding the number of recruiters for the RA will increase high-quality enlisted supply (Knapp et al., 2018), and estimates of the effects of recruiting resources on enlisted supply are similar for the USAR and ARNG when controlling for the number of prior-service accessions to those components (Tan, 1991). If these newly available recruiters generate cross-component contracts for recruits who otherwise would not have enlisted, the CRP could also improve overall recruiting efficiency. However, additional recruiters will generate meaningful increases in high-quality enlisted supply only if they are managed appropriately.

The production of high-quality contracts is dependent on the level of effort that recruiters allocate toward pursuing high-quality potential recruits. Polich, Dertouzos, and Press (1986) found that high-quality contract production for the RA (the active component) is three times more difficult than lower-quality contract production. If recruiters are not rewarded well enough to incentivize the extra effort involved in producing high-quality contracts, they may instead focus on lower-quality potential recruits to meet their missions. Similarly, recruiting missions can be a key determinant in the share of reserve enlistment contracts signed by personnel with no prior service, who require more effort to recruit (Tan, 1991). Numerous researchers have found that contract production responds to increases in recruiting missions and to individual incentive programs (Arkes and Cunha, 2015; Asch and Heaton, 2010; Knapp et al., 2018). However, the responsiveness falls as missions become more difficult to achieve (Dertouzos and Garber, 2006), and poorly designed incentive programs can have perverse effects, including a decline in the quality of enlistment contracts as deadlines for achieving goals draw closer (Asch and Heaton, 2010).

The conclusion of this line of literature is that recruiters distribute their effort in the manner required to make mission. If the Army wants recruiters to put effort toward a particular type of contract, especially one that requires a higher level of effort as cross-component contracts do, such contracts should be incorporated into recruiting missions. If recruiters perceive that it would be more work to write a cross-component contract than to just persuade a recruit to enlist in the recruiter's own component, then this could undermine the program. In other words, a potentially successful consolidated recruiting program could require the incorporation of cross-component contracts into recruiter missions, whether by allowing cross-component contracts to directly count toward recruiter or station missions or by setting explicit goals for cross-component contracts. At the same time, it is conceptually possible that requiring some number of cross-component contracts could have a different, perverse effect if recruiters might be forced to persuade a recruit to go into an ill-fitting alternative component only because the mission requires it.

Spillovers from Recruiting by Multiple Components

Previous researchers have noted that USAR recruiting can have either positive or negative *spillover* effects (flows of recruits between components) on high-quality contract production for the RA, especially when stations have missions for both the RA and USAR. Leads generated for USAR might end up signing contracts for the RA, and vice versa, raising the number of RA and USAR contracts at the station, particularly if those recruits would not have enlisted without having the choice to sign contracts for both components. This could increase the Army market share and efficiency if those leads and contracts would not have been generated without the dual recruiting mission. However, when operating from the same recruiting stations, both components compete for the same pool of high-quality potential enlistments, which could potentially decrease the number of RA or USAR contracts signed at a station while holding the total number of contracts signed at the station constant.

Prior research has examined whether stations that recruit for both the RA and USAR experience positive or negative spillover effects. A study conducted using data from FY 1999 to FY 2004 noted that stations with a USAR goal had a much lower likelihood of achieving station-level recruiting missions, which required making mission for both the RA and USAR. However, the existence of a reserve recruiting mission at a station did not have a large effect on RA recruiting in either direction, suggesting that the failure to meet mission was driven by the difficulty of achieving two separate recruiting goals rather than by negative spillovers (Dertouzos and Garber, 2006). More-recent models of enlisted supply suggest that raising USAR recruiting goals (and therefore recruiter effort allocated toward producing USAR contracts) decreases the number of high-quality enlistment contracts signed for the RA (Knapp et al., 2018). More recently, an analogous result was found for the effect of increasing the RA mission on USAR enlistment contracts (Orvis et al., forthcoming). Other researchers have recognized that other services' recruiting creates competition for the same pool of potential recruits. Some recruiting models explicitly account for the recruiting goals of other services when modeling the effects of different recruiting policies, typically finding that competition decreases each service's contract production (e.g., Warner, Simon, and Payne, 2001). Older work has also found limited effects of competition between reserve components on reserve enlistment supply in USAR and ARNG (Tan, 1991).

The CRP could create similar spillovers for RA and USAR recruiting or for ARNG recruiting. Large positive spillovers could occur if the ARNG is generating leads who prefer RA or USAR service but would not have been targeted by USAREC, or vice versa. However, negative spillovers could also occur because of increased competition between the three components for the station's limited supply of prospective recruits. If positive spillovers are larger than negative spillovers, the program would increase contract production and the Army market share and could also increase the efficiency of the recruiting enterprise by decreasing the number of appointments required to produce an enlistment contract. However, if negative spillovers are larger, the program would decrease contract production for the RA and USAR or for the ARNG. Given the theoretical ambiguity of the relative sizes of these two effects, a pilot program was required to test whether the addition of cross-component recruiting would help or harm Army recruiting.

Enlistment Bonuses and Education Benefits

A potential mechanism through which spillovers, both positive and negative, could operate involves the additional enlistment incentives offered to ARNG recruits in some states.[1] All three components offer enlistment bonuses for high-quality recruits and in-demand occupations, but some states provide additional enlistment bonuses for the ARNG—for example, for recruits not meeting the education credential and/or AFQT criteria for high-quality recruits or for those entering a combat Military Occupational Specialty (MOS). Similarly, members of all three components are eligible for the Post-9/11 GI Bill and other education benefits subject to certain conditions, but some states provide additional education benefits for ARNG personnel.

Prior research on active-component enlisted supply suggests that both enlistment bonuses and education benefits can channel high-quality recruits into particular occupations and services. Bonuses, in particular, have been shown to be effective for both skill channeling and market expansion. The effects of bonuses on skill channeling come from the fact that bonuses are often tied to a particular MOS, pulling recruits toward those that offer larger financial incentives (Polich, Dertouzos, and Press, 1986). The CRP could work similarly in that larger financial incentives from the ARNG could pull potential recruits from the RA and USAR to the ARNG. Similarly, early research on education benefits, conducted during a period when the

---

[1] Throughout this report, unless otherwise noted, the term *state* shall also refer to the District of Columbia, Commonwealth of Puerto Rico, and the territories of Guam and the Virgin Islands.

Army offered an additional education benefit to potential recruits relative to the other services, suggested that education benefits expand enlistments, and the effect is larger when larger education benefits are offered (Polich, Fernandez, and Orvis, 1982). The additional education benefits offered to ARNG personnel could have a similar effect, likely at the expense of the RA and USAR, if the CRP allows prospective recruits to learn about the available education benefits in different components.

There also is evidence that education benefits can create positive spillovers from ARNG recruiting to RA recruiting or from RA recruiting to USAR recruiting. Arkes and Kilburn (2005) found that states with education incentives for the National Guard have higher levels of both active and reserve enlisted supply. This suggests that, in addition to the relatively straightforward effects of ARNG education benefits on ARNG enlisted supply, a forward-looking prospective recruit might consider joining the RA with the plan to take advantage of state education benefits as a prior-service ARNG accession sometime in the future. However, the study acknowledges that education incentives in this context are potentially endogenous, which could bias the results; for instance, it might be the case that states offering education benefits for the ARNG are also those where youth have a higher propensity to serve. The 2+2+4 program (Buddin and Gresenz, 2004) combined two years of active duty followed by two years of selected reserve duty and additional time in the individual ready reserve; it significantly increased affiliations with the USAR.

Some prior research suggests that enlisted personnel typically have only limited information about even their own component's education benefits. For instance, the Post-9/11 GI Bill likely did not have a large effect on high-quality enlistments because of recruits' lack of understanding about the details of the program (Wenger et al., 2017). Research on the broader population of students has found that information frictions and high administrative burdens can prevent students from taking advantage of financial aid opportunities (Dynarski et al., 2018), suggesting that information frictions can prevent education benefits from being an effective policy lever. For education benefits to be an effective policy lever, enlisted personnel must understand which benefits are available and how to use them. If implemented properly, a consolidated recruiting program may have the potential to remove information frictions about the education benefits and bonuses available to recruits in all three components. The removal of information frictions could change the number of prospective recruits choosing the RA in either direction, as described in the previous paragraph, and might also expand the total number of high-quality enlistments across all of the components. However, for this to occur, recruiters at USAREC stations must understand the details of ARNG education benefits and be able to articulate those details to prospective recruits (and vice versa).

Recruit Eligibility Policies

A second channel through which spillovers could operate involves differences in recruit eligibility policies between USAREC and the ARNG. During the period of this pilot program, such differences involved such matters as greater eligibility for youth scoring below the 50th percentile on the AFQT or not having Tier 1 education credentials and the ability to overfill units in the ARNG. If prospective recruits do not currently realize that such differences exist, then under the CRP, recruits who are not eligible for the Regular Army and USAR but are eligible for the ARNG, or vice versa, could become more likely to enlist because of greater availability of information on their eligibility for each component. This also covers enlistments for active duty, which provide greater benefits and the opportunity to leave one's local area.

Implications of the Literature

In total, the relevant literature suggests that cross-component recruiting, such as that conducted under the CRP, may have the potential to improve overall Army recruiting efforts.[2] Specifically, consolidated recruiting can offer a wider selection of options to potential recruits; this could result in additional recruits (and, thus, increases in the Army's market share and efficiency, although these changes would not likely occur immediately). But these outcomes are dependent on recruiters understanding the different

---

[2] Given that the CRP is an Army program and that the other services approach recruiting in a somewhat different manner than the Army, we focus our literature review on research related to Army recruiting. However, many of the implications hold across the services (examples include the importance of recruiter incentives and the concern about cross-service and cross-component competition for the same pool of potential recruits).

options across the components, having incentives to write cross-component contracts (Oken and Asch, 1997; Desrosiers et al., 2019), and being able to balance separate recruiting goals. Also, the relative advantages and spill-overs to ARNG, USAR, and USAREC are unclear, but the existence of additional enlistment and educational incentives offered to ARNG recruits in some states could result in additional ARNG recruits at the expense of USAR or USAREC recruits. Of course, other evidence suggests that recruits often do not understand details of Army education benefits; if this is the case, then we would expect variation in education benefits to have small, negligible effects. While the research does not allow us to determine the likely effects of a cross-component recruiting program, it does suggest areas to examine, both as we analyze data on recruits and as we have discussions with recruiters and command leadership. Finally, it is worth noting that the NDAA language, which directs attention toward recruiters' ability to attract and place qualified candidates, as well as their reported satisfaction or challenges with the program and any discernable effects on recruiting efficiency, overlaps with areas that are most relevant to program success according to the literature.

Expected Outcomes

Above, we have documented the NDAA mandate that the Army conduct a three-year pilot program; during the program, Army recruiters were expected to recruit individuals into any of the three components. The idea of cross-component recruiting is not new (see, for example, Tan, 1991) but the genesis of this current pilot program can be traced to a report from the NCFA (2016). Both the report and the FY 2017 NDAA focus on increasing the effectiveness and efficiency of Army recruiting. Here, we combine infor-mation from these guiding documents with the literature on recruiting to consider how such a program could be expected to improve recruiting, what types of outcomes we might expect to see, and how we should think about measuring effectiveness.

The NCFA report (2016) recommended a multiyear pilot program to test the outcomes when recruiters from all three components were authorized to recruit individuals into any component. The report is explicit about the expected outcomes: Consolidated recruiting is viewed as a way of strengthening the Total Force and ensuring that the Army is seen as an integrated force (both externally and internally). But consolidated recruiting also is seen as a way to potentially strengthen enlistment production through improving match quality and to potentially decrease costs associated with recruiting. If match quality improves, this also would have the potential to decrease other longer-term costs, potentially through lower attrition or higher reenlistment rates (although such potential outcomes are not mentioned in the Future of the Army report).

The NDAA is explicit and detailed about the outcomes expected from the CRP. The NDAA names the following as key outcomes to be measured as part of the pilot program: effectiveness, that is the ability to attract qualified candidates; recruiting efficiency and costs; recruiter challenges; and recruiter satisfaction. (See the text of the NDAA provided earlier.) The first two outcomes could result from wider choices and better matches for potential recruits.

The literature on recruiting implies that cross-component recruiting may improve overall Army recruiting efforts, specifically by offering a wider range of options to potential recruits. Options could include a wider range of occupations (MOSs), a wider range of enlistment incentives, and even a wider range of eligibility criteria. But to realize these potential gains, recruiters must be incentivized to understand the range of options available and to write cross-component contracts. Finally, a consolidated model could result in negative outcomes caused by increased competition for recruits; such outcomes would depend heavily on how recruiters and stations were incentivized.

There is considerable overlap in outcomes that might be expected across these sources (the report, the NDAA, and the literature), but the sources also differ somewhat in their implications for measured outcomes. Broadly, consolidated recruiting is viewed as a method with the potential to improve recruiting by improving soldier-MOS match and perhaps to improve recruiter effectiveness. However, the report emphasizes an integrated (Total Force) Army as a potential outcome; this is not emphasized in the NDAA or in the recruiting literature. The literature does provide cautions about recruiter incentives; these cautions are not emphasized in the NDAA (or the report). Indeed, the literature provides several detailed reasons why a consolidated pilot might be unsuccessful: a lack of recruiter incentives, a lack of recruiter understanding of cross-component opportunities, and increased competition or incorrect missioning. Beyond what is mentioned in the literature, cross-component recruiting also requires additional coordination to ensure smooth hand-offs between components. Without such coordination and cooperation, cross-component recruiting could be ineffective. As discussed in Chapter Four, Army stakeholders raised concerns about this issue.

Taken as a whole, the information from the report, the NDAA, and the literature suggests that a complete evaluation of the CRP should include detailed measures of number and quality of contracts, early attrition (or other measures of match quality), and input from recruiters. These measures are included in our assessment of the CRP. We also measure cross-component contracts, to get a sense of the reasons for and scale of such contracts. But the broader measure presented in the report, the extent to which the program helps to integrate the Army into a Total Force, is not included. Measuring integration or collaboration across the components of the Army is certainly possible, but most methods of measuring this imprecise outcome would involve repeated surveys and strong assumptions to link a relatively small pilot recruiting program to overall collaboration measures.

The remainder of this report documents our final assessment of the pilot program. Chapter Two describes the pilot design and pilot activities. Chapter Three presents the results of our quantitative analyses through the end of the pilot program. Chapter Four presents the results of qualitative analysis undertaken throughout the pilot program examining recruiter and recruiting command experiences, satisfaction, and suggestions. Chapter Five summarizes these results, discusses their implications, and offers recommendations.

CHAPTER TWO

Pilot Design

The specifications for the design of the pilot test, including USAREC and ARNG test and comparison sites, outcome measures, and the quantification of results at the levels requested by the Army, were determined through a series of face-to-face meetings and telephonic conferences of the NCFA 38 Integrated Process Team (IPT) and Operational Planning Team (OPT) that included the study team; members of the office of the Headquarters Department of the Army (HQDA) Deputy Chief of Staff, G-1, Assistant Secretary of the Army (Manpower and Reserve Affairs) (ASA[M&RA]), and USAREC; and ARNG personnel. While the NDAA mandated the pilot test and some measures of effectiveness, it did not specify the research design. The IPT agreed on the goal of detecting a 5-percent change in enlistment contract production after the first year of the pilot test with 85-percent confidence. This is established as a two-tailed test, allowing for both positive and negative changes, as the focus in pilot tests should be not only on detecting benefits but also on detecting any potential harmful effects to determine whether national implementation should or should not be recommended. These decisions influenced the required number of test and comparison sites.

The USAREC–ARNG test and comparison site pairs were selected by the study team in coordination with USAREC and the ARNG through a rigorous, statistical analytical process using established principles for national recruiting pilot tests. To generate pairs of USAREC and ARNG recruiting locations, RAND Arroyo Center compared all possible USAREC station locations to all ARNG three-character Recruiting Station Identification Code (RSID) values. Recruiting organization is broken down by four characters to generate an RSID that covers recruiting in a defined geographic area. In USAREC, the first character of an RSID represents the brigade, the second the battalion, the third a Company, and the fourth an individual recruiting station (e.g., an Armed Services career center in a shopping mall). ARNG recruiters are organized differently. The first two characters of an ARNG RSID represent the state (e.g., TX or VA), the third represents a recruiting Team, and the fourth character represents an individual recruiter who is part of that Team.

To be eligible for inclusion in the pilot test, USAREC and ARNG pairs needed to be within the same state and within a 60-minute drive of each other (a USAREC Company had to have at least one such station). For all 600 possible USAREC and ARNG three-character RSID recruiting pairing locations that met these criteria, we then examined the USAREC and ARNG contracts written by each site to determine the geographic overlap of their enlistment contract footprints. Based on the number of contracts written and their overlap with respect to ZIP Codes, we created 195 best possible USAREC–ARNG three-character RSID pairs nationally, with *best* defined as a function of the pair's contract footprint overlap and overall contact production, such that each USAREC station or ARNG Team has only one match.

These 195 possible sites were used to select 14 test site pairs in participating states that were evenly distributed by inclusion criteria provided by USAREC and ARNG. This includes no more than three test sites per USAREC brigade and only one test site per state and USAREC battalion. Because the National Guard Bureau (NGB) does not have the authority to force states to participate in the pilot test, we were further limited by state ARNG decisions on participation. This resulted in only two test sites in the USAREC Sixth Brigade.

To ensure that the test sites were representative of the national recruiting environment, we also required a set of comparison sites that were balanced against the test sites. To achieve this, for each test-site pair, we found the three most similar USAREC-ARNG site pairs from the remaining 195 possible sites.[1] Similarity was defined according to a range of contract production–related balancing measures. The balancing measures

---

[1] We compared analysis plans using one to four comparison sites with respect to the effect of increasing the number on the size of the error term for the production comparison between the test sites versus comparison sites. After three comparison sites per

used were enlistment contracts written by the USAREC–ARNG pair from FY 2011–2016; open positions (vacancies) as of FY 2016 in reserve component units in the area served by the USAREC-ARNG pair; FY 2015 high-quality share of USAREC-ARNG pair contracts, defined as the percentage of recruits with both a Tier 1 education credential and an AFQT score at or above the 50th percentile of the national distribution; percentage of youth not white, non-Hispanic; number of youth ages 18–24; percentage of youth ages 18–24 enrolled in a four-year college; number of residents with a high school diploma; FY 2016 unemployment rate; FY 2016 per capita household income of the geographic areas served by a recruiting Company or Team; and share of in-state public tuition payable by ARNG education benefits.[2] Balancing was done at the test-site level to ensure the representativeness of sites selected but does not limit analysis. For all comparisons presented later in this report, differences are assessed between all test sites in the aggregate versus all comparison sites in the aggregate, not by individual test-comparison site pairs. The ratio-based Z-score approach described in Chapter Three applied to all test sites versus all comparison sites was how the outcome parameters agreed on by the IPT were to be measured (detect a 5-percent change in enlistment contract production after the first year of the pilot test with 85-percent confidence and only a 5-percent chance of obtaining a significant result by chance).

Of the 14 states having paired USAREC-ARNG sites meeting the inclusion criteria, 11 states agreed to actively participate in the pilot. Given three comparison site pairs for each test site pair, there were 33 comparison site pairs of USAREC recruiting Companies and ARNG recruiting Teams in the agreed-upon pilot test design (Table 2.1 and Table 2.2).

---

test site, the effect became minimal. Therefore, we used three comparison sites for each test site.

[2] Test and comparison sites are balanced based on minimizing the aggregate differences of these characteristics. Consequently, it is possible for test-comparison site pairs to differ notably on any single characteristic if they are very similar across all other characteristics. Alternative methods of balancing that punished large individual value differences were examined but did not produce substantively different results.

TABLE 2.1

Recruiting Company–Team Pairs in Consolidated Recruiting Program Pilot Test Location Information, Test Sites

USAREC Test Companies and Battalions		Army National Guard Test Teams and States		Company or Team Area
RSID	**Battalion**	**RSID**	**State**	
1B3	Baltimore	MDS	Maryland	Baltimore
1N6	Syracuse	NYA	New York	Rochester
3D4	Columbia (S.C.)	SCB	South Carolina	Greenville (S.C.)
3J1	Raleigh	NCP	North Carolina	Fayetteville
3T5	Baton Rouge	LAK	Louisiana	Baton Rouge
4J3	Oklahoma City	OKC	Oklahoma	Oklahoma City East
4K1	San Antonio	TXM	Texas	Austin
4P2	Phoenix	AZD	Arizona	Tucson
5J1	Milwaukee	WII	Wisconsin	Appleton
6H5	Portland (Ore.)	HI	Hawaii	Honolulu
6J6	Seattle	NVC, NVD	Nevada	Las Vegas

NOTE: Location information as of June FY 2019.

TABLE 2.2

Recruiting Company–Team Pairs in Consolidated Recruiting Pilot Test Location Information, Comparison Sites

USAREC Comparison Companies and Battalions		Army National Guard Comparison Teams and States		Company or Team Area
RSID	**Battalion**	**RSID**	**State**	
1G4	New York City	NYH	New York	Suffolk
1A5	Albany	CTA	Connecticut	Hartford
1O4	Richmond	VAB	Virginia	Lynchburg
3A7	Atlanta	TNO	Tennessee	Chattanooga
4E3	Houston	TXI	Texas	Houston North
4G9	Kansas City	MOH	Missouri	Mid-Missouri (Ft. Leonard Wood)

Table 2.2—Continued

USAREC Comparison Companies and Battalions		Army National Guard Comparison Teams and States		Company or Team Area
RSID	Battalion	RSID	State	
3J2	Raleigh	NCM	North Carolina	Greenville (N.C.)
6L4	Seattle	WAC	Washington	Tacoma
5D7	Columbus (OH)	OHG	Ohio	Cincinnati Metro
4P1	Phoenix	AZF	Arizona	Phoenix West (Glendale)
4K5	San Antonio	TXO	Texas	East San Antonio (Joint Base San Antonio, Tex.)
3T8	Baton Rouge	LAJ	Louisiana	Lafayette
5C5	Cleveland	OHF	Ohio	Marion (Ohio)
3D7	Columbia	SCD	South Carolina	Florence (S.C.)
3T9	Baton Rouge	LAC	Louisiana	Shreveport
3T4	Baton Rouge	TNV	Tennessee	Memphis
4C1	Dallas	TXD	Texas	McKinney
3J3	Raleigh	NCO	North Carolina	Raleigh
6F3	Los Angeles	CAJ	California	Long Beach
4G3	Kansas City	MOE	Missouri	Joplin (MO)
3A2	Atlanta	GAM	Georgia	Atlanta
3H2	Montgomery	FLA	Florida	Dothan (AL)
1K2	Mid-Atlantic (N.J.)	NJD	New Jersey	South Jersey (Cherry Hill)
1E9	Harrisburg	PAP	Pennsylvania	Lehigh Valley (Bethlehem)
5N5	Nashville	TNT	Tennessee	Clarksville (Tenn.)
4G1	Kansas City	MOA	Missouri	Greater Kansas City (Independence, Mo.)
5J6	Milwaukee	WIC	Wisconsin	Milwaukee
4K3	San Antonio	TXN	Texas	San Marcos
4P4	Phoenix	AZB	Arizona	Tempe

Table 2.2—Continued

USAREC Comparison Companies and Battalions		Army National Guard Comparison Teams and States		Company or Team Area
RSID	Battalion	RSID	State	
3N3	Tampa	FLF	Florida	Orlando
1D2	New England	NHA	New Hampshire	New Hampshire (Manchester)
3A6	Atlanta	GAI	Georgia	Peachtree City
3H6	Montgomery	ALE	Alabama	Huntsville

NOTE: Location information as of June FY 2019.

Using these locations, the pilot was well-balanced and came close to fully meeting assessment goals involving the statistical precision of tests and representativeness of pilot test sites compared with the national average (Table 2.3).[3] Based on average contract production in the years preceding the test (FY 2015–FY 2017), these 44 locations, 11 test and 33 comparison sites, were projected to produce sufficient contracts to be able to detect a

TABLE 2.3
Consolidated Recruiting Pilot Test Design Details

Factor	Test Sites	Comparison Sites	All Eligible Sites	All USAREC and ARNG Sites
Company-team pairs	11	33	138	195
Urban/suburban/ rural (%)	79/9/12	81/13/6	74/14/12	76/12/12
Average youth population	3,472	3,516	3,759	3,598
Average total contracts	584.47	503.99	461.09	406.33

[3] Pilot test sites also included additional modifications requested by participating states. In Nevada, the Team assigned to the pilot has since been split into two administrative units, both of which were included in the pilot to ensure balance remained. In Hawaii, all ARNG Teams were included in the pilot at the request of state leadership. As part of the process, the study team assessed the impact of these and other proposed changes on pilot balance and communicated concerns to USAREC and NGB as they arose.

5.5-percent change in production among the test sites after 12 months, reaching the targeted 5-percent level of precision after 19 months.

Test sites were also roughly representative of all possible sites in terms of their geographic distribution, youth population, and total production. Sites included USAREC stations and ARNG Teams that serve urban, suburban, and rural counties. Test and comparison sites were both slightly more urban than all possible sites, but, given that stations and Teams are allocated by population, this is not surprising. We also selected sites that were somewhat higher-producing on average than a typical recruiting Company-Team combination, roughly 120 additional contracts per year for test sites compared to eligible sites, or 40 additional contracts for comparison sites. This was done to allow the pilot test to achieve the desired statistical precision as quickly as possible while also meeting USAREC and ARNG restrictions on the number of overall test sites.

Pilot Activity

Beginning in June 2017, at the direction of the Secretary of the Army, a proof of concept for the pilot was executed between USAREC and the ARNG. The proof of concept worked to identify process, policy, information technology, and any other changes or instructions needed for implementation of a pilot program across the nation. Initial elements involved in the proof of concept were the Texas National Guard, Round Rock Center, and the U.S. Army 5th Recruiting Brigade's San Antonio Recruiting Company. Based on the results of this proof of concept, USAREC and the ARNG developed supporting training packages for implementation across the nation at the selected pilot locations. Mobile training teams trained all elements involved in the pilot during the period of October–December 2017, and USAREC posted the training materials on an internal internet site. After all elements were trained, full execution of the pilot under evaluation measures began on January 12, 2018. Two states, Texas and Arizona, temporarily suspended participation in the pilot program for the months of July–September 2018 at the request of ARNG state leadership. Both states resumed pilot participation in October 2018. Assessments in this report are made through June 2020, the end of the three-year pilot program period.

The NDAA language specifies that recruiters were to receive credit for cross-component contracts that they wrote during the pilot period regardless of the specific component for which they were written. USAREC and NGB established a set of business rules to determine how credit would be allocated to recruiters during the pilot program. The USAREC order establishing the pilot program specified that, when one of its recruiters wrote an ARNG contract, the station through brigade would receive USAR contract mission credit. This was done because at the time of the pilot program, USAREC did not assign a number of mission contracts required per month to individual recruiters but instead focused on the Company. In this formulation, when USAREC recruiters write a cross-component contract, their Company received credit toward its USAR mission. In contrast, ARNG recruiters were missioned individually and could receive credit toward their individual mission for each cross-component contract, in this case a soldier placed into the active-duty Army or USAR. Given that states, not the NGB, control their recruiting missions and practices, however, implementing this on the ground was left to each state for ARNG recruiters.

CHAPTER THREE

Quantitative Results

As part of the planning team with Army stakeholders, the researchers developed metrics of pilot program effectiveness drawn from the requirements of the NDAA language. These are the following: the ability of recruiters to attract and place qualified candidates, creating efficiency or reductions in recruiting costs, and recruiter satisfaction. For these overall metrics, we examined multiple measures to assess program effectiveness. Table 3.1 details the metrics, each measure, and the corresponding data sources.

TABLE 3.1

Pilot Evaluation Metrics, Measures, and Data Sources

Metric	Measure	Data Source
Attract and place qualified candidates	Total contract production	All Army contracts
Attract and place qualified candidates	High-quality contract production	High-quality Army contracts
Attract and place qualified candidates	Army market share	Army contracts/all-service contracts
Efficiency or reduced costs	Ratio of appointments made to contracts signed	Recruiter appointments/enlistment contracts
Efficiency or reduced costs	Delayed Entry Program (DEP) attrition and reserve component (RC) attrition prior to completion of MOS training	RA analyst file (contracts), Total Army Personnel Database (attrition), Army Training Requirements and Resources System database (training taken and training completed)
Recruiter satisfaction with program	Recruiter satisfaction with program	Recruiter focus groups, NGB input, HQ USAREC input

When examining the ability of recruiters to attract and place qualified applicants, we focus on contract production. This includes overall production of contracts within a test-pair area, as well as limiting analysis to the production of high-quality recruits. Recruits are considered *high-quality* if they have both a high school diploma (or equivalent Tier I education credential) and score above the national average on the AFQT (top 50 percentiles, i.e., AFQT categories I-IIIA). We also examined overall Army market share, the proportion of contracts in a geographic area written into the Army as a percentage of all military service contracts from that area, as another measure of ability to attract and place qualified candidates.

Other metrics focused on efficiencies in the recruiting process. One efficiency measure focused on the ratio of recruiter appointments to contracts produced, with a small ratio being more efficient. Others examine the training completion rates of reserve components (RC) soldiers and the DEP attrition rates of active-duty soldiers. We describe each analysis and the data in greater detail in the corresponding sections below.

We also undertook a detailed analysis of any cross-component contracts—that is, soldiers written into the ARNG by a USAREC recruiter or soldiers written into the RA or USAR by an ARNG recruiter—to explore why that soldier might have chosen a cross-component enlistment. This analysis was not required by the NDAA but was thought of as valuable by IPT members in assessing the program. Possible reasons considered included different MOSs available in another component (e.g., a combat MOS in the ARNG that was not available in the USAR); better incentives in an alternative component; a difference in waiver or eligibility policies in another component, or the opportunity to leave an area or find full-time versus part-time employment and related job benefits in another component.

Ability of Recruiters to Attract and Place Qualified Candidates

As discussed in the NCFA recommendation and the NDAA, part of the motivation for the pilot program was to improve the ability of recruiters to match recruits to the best opportunity for them while maintaining or increasing the number and the quality of candidates recruited into the Army. To assess the ability of recruiters to attract and place qualified candidates, we focused on contract production and leveraged the experimental nature of the pilot design for our analyses. Data were drawn from the Army Data Warehouse and include information on all contracts signed by recruiters affiliated with pilot or comparison sites. We produced a test statistic that is a ratio comparing changes in the test areas during the test period to an equally long baseline period, divided by the analogous ratio for the comparison areas. The error term for the ratio is the square root of the sum of the reciprocals of the contracts written in each of the four combinations of sites and time periods. Subtracting one from the ratio and dividing by the error term produces a z-statistic (whose values follow the standard normal distribution, with a mean of zero and a standard deviation of one).[1]

We make two comparisons—the comparison of test sites during the pilot period to themselves at an earlier time and then to the comparison sites—to isolate the impact of the pilot test from possible residual differences in the test versus comparison sites and from possible differences in the recruiting environment more broadly that could occur during the test period relative to the baseline period. In the absence of program effects, the mathematically expected value of the test site–to–comparison site ratio is 1.00. The test can detect both positive and negative effects, represented here by a ratio larger or smaller than one, respectively. To be statistically meaningful, the probability of obtaining the observed results by chance must be less than 0.05 (5 percent).[2]

Tables 3.2 and 3.3 show the final results through the end of the pilot program, June 2020, for overall contracts written and high-quality contracts written by the test and comparison sites during the pilot test and baseline periods; the ratio of the number of contracts written by the test sites

---

[1] An alternative method to test these differences is to use a difference-in-differences regression approach that directly compares each test site to its comparison sites, rather than comparing all test sites versus all comparison sites. We estimated this regression for both contract production and high-quality contract production; the results showed no statistically significant impact of the pilot program.

[2] A difference associated with less than a 10-percent probability of obtaining the result by chance but 5 percent or greater of it being a chance result is considered marginally statistically significant.

TABLE 3.2

Total Contract Production

All Army Components	Contract Totals	Calculations	
Test sites: baseline period	22,256	Test site ratio	0.67
Test sites: test period	14,929	Comparison site ratio	0.68
Comparison sites: baseline period	54,482	Test site: comparison site ratio	0.99
Comparison sites: test period	36,807	Error term	0.01
Total contracts	128,474	Z-statistic	−0.57
		P-level	0.57

NOTE: All p-values are two-tailed.

TABLE 3.3

High-Quality Contract Production

All Army Components	Contract Totals	Calculations	
Test sites: baseline period	12,589	Test site ratio	0.69
Test sites: test period	8,629	Comparison site ratio	0.68
Comparison sites: baseline period	30,993	Test site : comparison site ratio	1.01
Comparison sites: test period	20,996	Error term	0.02
Total contracts	73,207	Z-statistic	0.71
		P-level	0.48

NOTE: All p-values are two-tailed.

during the test period to the number written during the baseline period; the analogous ratio for the comparison site contracts; the ratio of the test site ratio to the comparison site ratio; and the probability of obtaining this last ratio in the absence of a true difference between the test and comparison sites, given the numbers of contracts shown on the left side. Here, the test site–to–comparison site ratio is near 0.99 for overall contracts and approximately 1.00 for high-quality contracts, with associated probabilities of obtaining the results by chance in the absence of a true difference of 0.57 (57 percent) and 0.48 (48 percent). Therefore, as noted earlier, the small difference in production of enlistment contacts between the test and comparison sites is not statistically meaningful at p < 0.05. That is to say, the assessment of the pilot did not provide evidence of a statistically meaningful impact on contract or high-quality contract production.[3]

Beyond the production of contracts overall, another important metric of the pilot test was the impact on the Army's market share relative to other services in the U.S. Department of Defense. Here, the main outcome of interest was the percentage of contracts that were written into any component of the Army (active duty, USAR, ARNG)—the Army's share—of all contracts written into any service or component (Air Force, Army, Marine Corps, Navy). As part of the goal to increase market share, the overall goal was to also increase the total number of contracts written for *any* service, so that an Army increase in market share would not be achieved by taking contracts away from other services, which compete for enlistees.[4]

To examine differences, we used a multivariate regression with a similar logic to the test statistic above. In this case, we regressed the monthly market share, expressed as the percentage of contracts written into the Army among the total contracts written into all services and components, controlling for whether the site was a test site or comparison site, whether the percentage was for a month in the test period or baseline period, the month of the year when the market share was observed, and whether the market share percentage occurred for a test site during the test period. This regression performed the same comparisons as above: test sites during the test period to prior versions of themselves and to the comparison sites. In this formulation, it is

---

[3] To check for differences in time trends between the test and comparison sites within the baseline and test periods, we used a continuous term for month. We prefer month-based time terms given known—and relatively consistent year over year—impacts of months on contract production. We ultimately found no evidence, either in the regressions or graphically, of a time trend that is unique to the test sites during the test period. Any observed fixed effects of time appear to equally affect the comparison sites, suggesting that they are more likely related to changes in the recruiting environment (e.g., a lowering unemployment rate for much of the test period) that are unmeasured by our simple models rather than a change related to the pilot test.

[4] We note that there is no expectation that the results of this analysis would have a clear level of statistical precision, since increasing market share was not one of the criteria used to design the number of test and comparison sites.

the interaction term of test site by test period that assesses whether the test sites performed differently than the comparison sites during the test period. As shown in Table 3.4, the coefficient for the interaction term between test sites and test period (isolating the impact of the test itself) is –0.51. This term indicates that, holding constant test site and test period differences, test sites reduced their market share by 0.5 percentage points during the test period. The "t statistic" for the interaction term is –0.04, with an associated probability of obtaining the results by chance in the absence of a true difference between the test and comparison sites of 0.33. In other words, such a result might be expected to occur by chance roughly one-third of the time. Therefore, as noted earlier, we cannot conclude in a statistically significant manner that the pilot program was associated with an Army gain or loss in market share through the completion of the program in June 2020.

Increased Efficiency

Another goal of the pilot test is to increase recruiting efficiency, and, thus, possibly to reduce recruiting cost over the longer term. One metric of efficiency is the ratio of appointments made by recruiters to the contracts they produced. If the pilot program allows recruiters to be more efficient, they would need fewer appointments to achieve the same number of contracts. Table 3.5 shows the results of a multivariate regression that uses the same format as above with Army market share. Again, we are focused on the interaction term, which assesses whether the test sites performed differently than the comparison sites during the test period after accounting for the other factors. As shown in Table 3.5, through June 2020, the interaction term of test-period and test site is 0.28, suggesting that during the test-period test

TABLE 3.4
Army Market Share (Converted to Percentages)

	Interaction Coefficient	T-statistic	P-value
January 2018 to June 2020			
Market share	–0.51	–0.04	0.33

NOTE: All p-values are two-tailed. The comparison for the first test-site pair covers June 2017 to June 2020.

TABLE 3.5

Mean Appointment/Contract Ratio

	Interaction Coefficient	T-statistic	P-value
January 2018 to June 2020			
Appointments/contracts	0.28	0.84	0.40

NOTE: All p-values are two-tailed.

sites required 0.28 additional appointments per contract holding constant other factors. The "*t* statistic" for the interaction term is 0.84 with an associated probability of obtaining the results by chance in the absence of a true difference between the test and comparison sites of 0.40.[5] Therefore, we cannot conclude in a statistically significant manner that the pilot program was associated with a gain or loss in recruiting efficiency through the end of the program.

Another efficiency-based metric for assessing the performance of the pilot program involves whether DEP attrition is less or greater for cross-component recruits placed into the RA by the ARNG compared with USAREC recruits for active duty. This measure concerns the increased (decreased) recruiting costs associated with replacing DEP losses.

These results are shown in Table 3.6. Examining DEP losses, we found that 4.87 percent of contracts written by USAREC recruiters in test sites during the test period resulted in a loss. That is, the recruit (or recruiter) canceled the contract before shipping to basic training. Of the cross-component contracts written by ARNG recruiters at the same time and locations, losses occurred for 2.6 percent of contracts. When examined statistically, these numbers are not meaningfully different, with a p-value of 0.34. By necessity, this analysis was conducted on a limited population of contracts—those contracting at least 12 months before the end of the pilot program, to allow recruits time to exit the DEP before training naturally.

---

[5] As a further specification test, we also considered a model that predicted the natural log of appointments conducted, rather than the ratio of appointments to contracts. This specification may be preferred as the point estimates of the model are clearer to interpret but loses the connection to contract production gained by including signed contracts in the ratio. This model did not produce substantively different results, indicating no statistically significant change in Army recruiting efficiency.

TABLE 3.6

Cross-Component Versus Same-Component Contract DEP Status Comparisons

T-Test Analysis	USAREC Mean	ARNG Mean	Difference (ARNG minus USAREC)	T-statistic	P-value
DEP loss, ARNG into RA versus USAREC to RA	4.87%	2.60%	–2.27%	–0.92	0.34

NOTE: All p-values are two-tailed. USAREC N = 8,688 contracts, ARNG N = 77 contracts. Analysis is based on data through March 2020, given limited ability of new training starts in Spring 2020 due to COVID-19.

A third efficiency measure, related to training, involves whether attrition from RC units prior to training completion is different for cross-component versus same-component contracts into the ARNG. Table 3.7 shows the results of this analysis. We examined the rates of having completed MOS training (either Advanced Individual Training [AIT] or One Station Unit Training [OSUT]) for USAREC (cross-component) versus ARNG (same-component) contracts into the ARNG.[6] As discussed earlier, unlike active-duty soldiers, those who enlist in the ARNG or USAR (there were only two contracts written by the ARNG for the USAR) do not go into a DEP but instead are immediately placed in a unit. To be of value to that unit, a new soldier must complete MOS training. We compared the rate of having completed such training between cross-component and same-component contracts into the ARNG.[7]

Similar to the DEP analysis above, these analyses focused on a limited pool of contracts that allowed sufficient time to pass for us to observe soldier

---

[6] An analogous case of ARNG cross-component enlistees into the USAR versus USAREC recruits into the USAR is logically possible. However, it was not actually possible given that only two cross-component contracts were written into the USAR through the end of the pilot program, rendering statistical analysis of that combination impossible.

[7] *Same-component ARNG soldiers* are restricted to those soldiers enlisted by test site ARNG Teams in the test period who entered a unit that received at least one cross-component soldier. We restricted our analyses to the same units to avoid any confounding unit-level effects given that training is arranged by each unit individually.

TABLE 3.7

Cross-Component Versus Same-Component ARNG MOS Training Completion

Completion Time AIT/OSUT

Completed AIT/OSUT within 12 months of service ARNG into ARNG versus USAREC into ARNG		ARNG into ARNG	USAREC into ARNG
	Failed/did not start training	35	16
	Completed training	124	59
		Chi-square = 0.01	P-value = 0.91
Completed AIT/OSUT within 15 months of service ARNG into ARNG versus USAREC into ARNG		ARNG into ARNG	USAREC into ARNG
	Failed/did not start training	31	15
	Completed training	145	65
		Chi-square = 0.05	P-value= 0.83

NOTE: All p-values are two-tailed. Training analysis is based on data through June 2020 with exceptions accounting for limited ability of new training starts in Spring 2020 due to COVID-19.

training outcomes.[8] Within the 12 months time frame, 35 soldiers written into the ARNG by ARNG recruiters failed or had not started training, compared with 16 from their cross-component counterparts. The remainder, 124 and 59, respectively, had completed training by that point. Assessing the differences in passage rates by recruiter type indicates no statistically

---

[8] To assess training results, we first defined the portion of soldiers who had enough time in service such that we would reasonably expect an RC soldier to complete training. For most, this is within 12 months. We modeled training within 15 months as well to acknowledge that some soldiers who will ultimately be trained take slightly over a year to finish. For this population, we pulled all training records available in the Army's Training Requirements and Resource System, the Army training system of record, and compared them with existing qualification and attrition data from the Total Army Personnel Database–National Guard.

significant difference in training rates after 12 months of service time. Repeating these results with an additional three months, allowing soldiers more time to have completed MOS training but reducing the pool of soldiers we have available to make comparisons, also indicates no statistically significant results.

Cross-Component Contracts

In addition to these overall measures of effectiveness required by the NDAA, we examined recruits who signed cross-component contracts in more detail. While this analysis was not formally required by the NDAA, it was thought of as valuable for assessing the pilot program by study IPT members. There are many reasons a potential recruit could choose one component over another; having analysis to systematically examine patterns in component decisions across the pilot program helps decisionmakers and stakeholders understand what recruits are looking for when they sign cross-component contracts. One reason a recruit might sign a cross-component contract is to gain a position in a MOS area that is not offered by the same component. This is especially common in the RC for two reasons. First, RC soldiers are limited in the MOSs that they can join by the geographic distribution of USAR or ARNG units in their area. For example, it is impossible for a recruit to sign up to be a Military Police soldier if there are no units with Military Police positions in his or her area or state. Second, the USAR is structured to be primarily combat support (CS) and combat service support (CSS), with relatively few combat arms (CA) units, such as infantry or armor, among its units. This is not the case with the ARNG, which has many combat arms units. Thus, recruits might be motivated to switch components to find a different job. Table 3.8 presents the results of tests comparing cross-component contracts with their same-component counterparts. The first portion of the table shows the distribution of contracts written by USAREC recruiters into the RA versus ARNG recruiters into the RA, by MOS position type. For example, USAREC recruiters wrote 1,757 RA CA contracts, 1,935 RA CS contracts, and 2,596 RA CSS contracts. When we compare this distribution with those cross-component contracts written by ARNG recruiters, we cannot conclude in a statistically significant manner at the $p < 0.05$ level

TABLE 3.8

Cross-Component Versus Same-Component Contract Comparisons

Alternative Career Management Field Area

ARNG into RA versus USAREC into RA		USAREC into RA	ARNG into RA
	CA	1,757	20
	CS	1,935	20
	CSS	2,596	20
		Chi-square = 1.66	**P-value** = 0.44

USAREC into ARNG versus ARNG into ARNG		ARNG into ARNG	USAREC into ARNG
	CA	1,086	35
	CS	1,263	37
	CSS	1,626	47
		Chi-square = 0.46	**P-value** = 0.79

NOTE: All p-values are two-tailed.

that there was an overall difference through June 2020 in the distributions by MOS occupation type. This is also true of the reverse situation: recruits placed in the ARNG by USAREC recruiters compared with ARNG recruits placed by ARNG recruiters.[9]

Table 3.9 continues our examination of the MOS types sought by cross-component recruits, specifically testing the hypothesis that those recruits entering the ARNG with a USAREC recruiter might be seeking CA positions not available in the USAR. In the first row, we see that roughly 27 percent of USAREC soldiers put into the ARNG entered CA MOS positions, compared with roughly 30 percent for ARNG into ARNG contracts. Based on this difference, roughly 3 percent, we cannot conclude in a statistically

---

[9]   As with the earlier RC component training analysis, we were unable to conduct the reverse of this analysis (ARNG into USAR) because of the limited number of cross-component contracts into the USAR.

TABLE 3.9

Additional Cross-Component Versus Same-Component Contract Comparisons

T-Test Analysis	ARNG Mean	ARNG N	USAREC Mean	USAREC N	Difference (ARNG minus USAREC)	T-statistic	P-value
Cross-Component Contracts, USAREC into ARNG							
CA USAREC into ARNG versus ARNG into ARNG	29.69%	4,098	27.42%	128	2.27%	0.56	0.57
Bonus amounts, USAREC into ARNG versus USAREC into USAR	$7,988	1,868	$5,637	128	$2,351	3.71	0.00
Bonus amounts, USAREC into ARNG versus USAREC into USAR–high-quality only	$9,430	1,003	$8,722	79	$708	0.86	0.39
Bonus amounts, USAREC into ARNG versus USAREC into USAR–non–high-quality only	$5,663	865	$2,059	49	$3,604	5.06	0.00
Bonus amounts, USAREC into ARNG versus USAREC into USAR–combat MOS	$11,184	115	$3,791	38	$7,393	5.80	0.00
Bonus amounts, USAREC into ARNG versus USAREC into USAR–non-combat MOS	$6,639	1,753	$5,758	90	$880	–1.18	0.24
Waivers, USAREC into ARNG versus USAREC into USAR–non-administrative waiver	3.30%	1,761	4.54%	121	–1.24%	0.64	0.52

Table 3.9—Continued

T-Test Analysis	ARNG Mean	ARNG N	USAREC Mean	USAREC N	Difference (ARNG minus USAREC)	T-statistic	P-value
Cross-Component Contracts, ARNG into USAREC							
CA ARNG into RA versus USAREC into RA	35.00%	60	29.20%	6,473	5.80%	0.98	0.33
Bonus amounts, ARNG into RA versus USAREC into RA	$3,700	60	$5,076	10,576	–$1,376	–1.22	0.22
Waivers, ARNG into RA versus USAREC into RA–non-administrative waiver	0.00%	54	4.58%	9904	–4.58%	1.61	0.11

NOTE: All p-values are two-tailed.

significant manner at the $p < 0.05$ level that there was an overall difference through June 2020 in the prevalence of CA positions between cross-component and same-component recruits.

Another reason a soldier might sign a cross-component contract is to receive a larger financial incentive for doing so. Different components offer different bonuses for enlisting—on the ARNG side, this can even vary by state—leading to potential differences in the level of financial support that a recruit can receive for enlisting. For these analyses, we compared the financial incentives that cross-component recruits into the ARNG (those placed by USAREC recruiters) received relative to the average bonus levels of recruits placed into the USAR by USAREC recruiters across the same test sites. In effect, we were testing what bonus cross-component recruits would have received if a recruiter had been unable to place them into the ARNG but they had persisted with enlisting into an RC unit. In this comparison, we found that USAR recruits received an average of $5,600 in bonuses, while the cross-component recruits received slightly under $8,000 in bonuses. This difference, of roughly $2,350 dollars, is statistically significant and substantive, representing an increase of over 40 percent. It indicates that one possible reason recruits signed a cross-component contract could be that the ARNG offered them a better bonus than the USAR.

More specifically, we further broke out this analysis by two factors commonly associated with bonuses—recruit quality and job type. Eligibility for bonuses is often linked to a recruit being *high-quality*—as defined by both having a high school diploma and scoring in the upper 50 percentiles of the AFQT. We found no statistically meaningful difference among high-quality recruits, but owing to differences in component needs and/or policies, recruits who did not have a Tier 1 high school diploma or scored below the 50th percentile on the AFQT received significantly higher bonuses, almost $4,000 greater, if they joined the ARNG rather than the USAR.

The bonus difference is even more dramatic for cross-component recruits enlisting into combat positions. In our sample, those joining CA units in the ARNG as cross-component contracts received a bonus that was more than $7,000 larger, on average, than those joining the USAR. Combat recruits are normal targets of larger MOS bonuses, including when enlisting for active duty, and the USAR has very few such units—whereas the ARNG has many. Greater financial incentives offered by the ARNG to non–high-quality recruits and to recruits into combat positions thus appear to be reasons recruits may opt for cross-component contracts.

Other reasons considered for why recruits might opt for a cross-component contract included easier eligibility or waiver policies in one component versus another. Our analyses, presented in Table 3.9, do not offer evidence in favor of this hypothesis, even though a number of recruiters reported this as a reason for cross-component contracts. Our data indicate that we cannot conclude in a statistically significant manner at the $p < 0.05$ level that there was an overall difference through the end of the pilot program in waiver rates between cross-component and same-component contracts. Finally, another hypothesized reason for signing a cross-component contract (including some recruiters' reports of their discussions with potential recruits) involved recruits' desire for a full-time job or to leave a dangerous area or one with limited opportunities. Active duty compared to the part-time local nature of RC service would provide such an opportunity. There is some evidence for this, considering that all but two of the cross-component contracts written by ARNG recruiters were into active-duty service rather than reserve service in the USAR. It also should be noted that the ARNG has very generous in-state college tuition benefits. The benefits vary by state and over time, but they very often are much larger than what the USAR can offer. The benefits provide substantial reason for cross-component contracts into the ARNG.

CHAPTER FOUR

Qualitative Results: Conversations with Recruiters and Command Leadership

We assessed the challenges and opportunities associated with recruiting individuals into a different component through discussions with multiple groups of stakeholders. We conducted recruiter focus group discussions during the first two years of the pilot period, and, at the end of the program, we conducted discussions with command leadership and interviews with recruiters from the most successful test sites in writing cross-component contracts. Appendix A includes our protocol, as well as detailed notes from each set of discussions. Here, we summarize the program strengths and challenges as perceived by the stakeholders.

Positive Aspects, or Strengths, of the CRP

Across stakeholders, there was general agreement that the CRP held at least the potential to benefit both the Army and recruits. *The main benefit to Army recruits was thought to be access to more, and more varied, opportunities through a single recruiter.* Stakeholders mentioned numerous specific examples, such as allowing a USAREC recruiter to offer access to part-time service in combat jobs in the ARNG (given that few such options exist in the USAR), allowing better or broader options for recruits who might need a waiver or who have low test scores, allowing applicants working with an ARNG recruiter to join the RA with a full-time job and thus leave a dangerous hometown or one that lacked opportunity, and allowing a recruit to change components in the middle of the recruiting process without starting over. Stakeholders also noted that potential recruits do not understand the difference between the components, thus making the "one-stop shop" aspect of consolidated recruiting especially valuable.

Another positive aspect of the program mentioned across stakeholders was the *establishment of stronger relationships between the components*. The program opened lines of communication between the ARNG and USAREC at the Company-Team level. On the field side, the program led to increased levels of communication and coordination among recruiters. Some noted that increased coordination allowed them to work together—for example, by having two Army representatives at key events; they reported that this made recruiting easier. These relationships are viewed as valuable and are expected to persist.

A different sort of advantage mentioned by stakeholders is that the program served to *increase community awareness*—for example, by allowing USAREC to capitalize on the local recognition and networks that ARNG recruiters had built over time.

Finally, recruiters at the locations that wrote the largest number of cross-component contracts noted that *the program helped them to make their mission*. These recruiters noted specifically that USAREC to ARNG contracts counted toward the USAR mission (although see the discussion of issues related to incentives below); also, the program was perceived to have facilitated recruiting for the RA.

Negative Aspects, or Challenges, of the CRP

All stakeholders mentioned multiple negative aspects of the CRP. As is the case for the positive aspects of the program, their concerns can be divided into categories or themes. The negative aspect that was mentioned most often concerned *lack of information*. Stakeholders who discussed this issue tended to mention either *a need for additional, ongoing training or for better information via websites*, or both.

Successful cross-component recruiting requires that recruiters have broad knowledge of opportunities and incentive packages across the Army's components, but also that the recruiters understand variation in the Army's policies and practices related to recruiting. For example, there are numerous differences in how USAREC and the ARNG process applicants. This issue appears to be especially problematic when opportunities, incentives, policies, or procedures change, as well as when recruiters turn over. But stakeholders also mentioned other aspects of information that posed challenges—for example, *recruiters needed to understand many specifics about the other component beyond benefits and bonuses (structure, assignment policy, etc.).* And each component needed to trust that other recruiters could describe opportunities and benefits accurately. Finally, some stakeholders noted that there was limited initial awareness of the program, and that *initial training was insufficient.* Some who arrived on station after the initial training were not offered training on the CRP at all (in response to this feedback, USAREC conducted a second round of training at the test sites and updated its online information site provided for recruiters to get the latest information about the program during 2019).

Stakeholders frequently mentioned issues related to using websites to obtain accurate and up-to-date information on opportunities and recruiting processes. In particular, recruiters struggled because they could not find all the necessary information on a single, user-friendly website. Multiple state-level differences within the ARNG websites posed a particular challenge, as did difficulties accessing all relevant information on ARNG websites. But ARNG recruiters also struggled to obtain necessary access to the USAREC website. Teams and leadership did make progress in resolving these issues throughout the pilot program.

Another strong theme among the negative aspects mentioned by stakeholders concerned *recruiter incentives.* Beyond the question of whether recruiters had access to all the information they needed to explain the complete set of options and write cross-component contracts, writing cross-component contracts took time away from other recruiter efforts. If recruiters do not receive credit for contracts, or if the incentives do not appear well-aligned to recruiters, recruiters are unlikely to work hard to complete cross-component contracts. Multiple stakeholders raised the issue of recruiter incentives. All these comments focused on how recruits were counted toward goals and mission. In the 2018–2019 focus groups, recruiters expressed concern over not receiving credit for cross-component contracts, because most maintained their component-specific contract missions. HQ

USAREC similarly raised the issue of confusion about credit, mentioning that recruiters had initially believed that credit would go all the way through the chain of command—but when USAR credit was awarded only at the Company level, USAREC recruiters had little incentive to enlist soldiers into ARNG. USAREC also did not receive credit for contracts into the RA/USAR written by ARNG recruiters. This exact point—credit for contracts into the RA/USAR written by ARNG recruiters—was also mentioned by recruiters at the sites that wrote the highest number of cross-component contracts; they noted that when ARNG recruiters wrote contracts into RA, these did not count against the RA mission. Furthermore, ARNG recruiters received credit for contracts written by USAREC recruiters only at the state level. The inability of USAREC recruiters to receive credit at the station level or USAREC and ARNG recruiters to have a mission reduction based on the cross-component contracts written were disincentives to spend time on cross-component contracts, since they still needed to meet their own organization's missions.

Stakeholders also mentioned *lack of a policy directing how handoffs between components should occur.* This caused instances of losing track of recruits and whether their enlistment packages were properly completed before the cross-component recruits arrived at the Military Entrance Processing Station (MEPS). The handoff confusion relatedly impeded interactions with the recruits prior to the date of their enlistment or transfer to ARNG units, which was reported to have hampered the process of building relationships with them and preparing them for service.

Finally, in some cases, there were more fundamental problems—in particular, *some recruiters did not buy into the potential for gain from cross-component recruiting.* Some viewed the program as an interruption or as requiring too large an investment of time for the payoff; others viewed cross-component recruiters as competitors and did not break away from this mentality.

CHAPTER FIVE

Review of Final Results of the Consolidated Recruiting Program Pilot Test and Their Implications

Consistent with the recommendations of the NCFA, the FY 2017 NDAA mandated a pilot test of a CRP for at least three years. The Army conducted this pilot test during June 2017–June 2020. In this report, we discussed the relevant literature, the design of the pilot, measurable effects on recruiting, and feedback from stakeholders. In the absence of a statistically meaningful effect on contract production or recruiting efficiency and given certain stakeholder concerns, the Army decided to terminate the pilot program after the third year. While the study team concluded that continuation of the pilot was not warranted and that the obstacles to success were not likely to be overcome in the near term, we briefly summarize each aspect of the project in this chapter and provide some recommendations that could strengthen a future consolidated recruiting effort.

Literature and Design of Pilot

The existing literature on recruiting suggests the potential for a consolidated recruiting program that could increase quality and/or market expansion, as well as some cautionary notes. First, the literature suggests that potential recruits who are considering entry into the active or reserve components have similar determinants—in each case, bonuses and education benefits, as well as recruiter effort and advertising, appear to have broadly similar effects. Coupled with the variation in opportunities and benefits across components, this finding of similar determinants suggests that a consolidated recruiting program has the potential to increase the supply of recruits and to increase the efficiency of Army recruiting efforts. However, the literature clearly indicates the importance of incentivizing recruiters; especially in the case of high-quality recruits, production is tied to recruiter effort. Incentivizing recruiters could occur through a variety of mechanisms, but recruiting mission is the mechanism that is most often mentioned. The *spillover effects* (or the net flow of recruits between components) are less clear from the literature; for example, cross-component recruiting efforts could result in a net flow of recruits into or out of the RA, depending on the specific circumstances. The need for recruiters to have a good understanding of the options available to recruits is not explicit in the literature, but it is assumed.

In the case of the CRP, the pilot program was designed carefully and precisely, and the sites appear to have adhered to this design. The design resulted in balanced test and comparison sites; paired together, these sites were representative of recruiting sites more broadly and were expected to reveal differences that could be linked to the pilot program. For 11 test site pairs of USAREC Companies and ARNG Teams and 33 comparison site pairs, we assessed three measures of recruiters' ability to attract candidates: total enlistment contracts, high-quality contracts, and Army market share (Army enlistment contracts as a percentage of all services' enlistment contracts written in area).[1] Another program goal was to increase recruiting efficiency, thus possibly reducing recruiting cost over the longer term. The ratio of appointments made by recruiters to the contracts produced represents one such metric of efficiency. Another efficiency-based metric involves two measures of attrition: (1) whether DEP attrition is less or greater for cross-component recruits placed into the RA by the ARNG compared with USAREC recruits for active duty, which concerns the increased (decreased) recruiting costs associated with replacing DEP losses; and (2) whether attrition from RC units prior to training completion is greater for USAREC recruits into the ARNG relative to ARNG recruits into the ARNG,

---

[1] By agreement with the other members of the process teams that defined the outcome measures for the pilot program, the market share goal was to increase the total number of contracts written into the Army while not taking contracts away from other services.

which affects both recruiting and training costs (because training losses can occur during training or between courses, resulting in lost training investments). We also examined the number of and reasons for cross-component contracts.

Effects of the Pilot on Recruiting

The measured differences in contracts, market share, and efficiency between test and comparison sites were relatively small and were not statistically significant. Thus, we cannot state that the program affected contracts, market share, or efficiency in a statistically or substantively meaningful way. Comparison of cross-component versus same-component contracts with respect to MOS area (i.e., combat, CS, CSS), enlistment incentives, and part-time service versus active duty showed some statistically significant differences. These indicate that cross-component recruits from USAREC into the ARNG received higher enlistment bonuses than recruits into the USAR. This disparity was driven by bonuses for recruits into combat positions and lower-quality recruits (those without Tier 1 education credentials and/or who did not score in AFQT Categories I-IIIA). This is consistent with at least some recruits having access to preferable benefits (bonuses, in this case) as a result of cross-component recruiting but does not suggest an increase in quality or a market expansion effect.

All but two cross-component recruits from the ARNG to USAREC enlisted for active duty. Recruiters attributed this to the recruits' desire to leave the area or secure a full-time job and related benefits.

We found no meaningful (statistical) difference in DEP attrition between ARNG cross-component contracts into the RA versus USAREC enlistees into the RA, or, by analogy, on completing Initial Entry Training by 12 or 15 months following enlistment among USAREC cross-component contracts into the ARNG versus ARNG contracts into the ARNG. Likewise, we found no difference in MOS area between cross-component and same-component contracts.

Summary of CRP Strengths and Weaknesses

We have three sources of information to assess the strengths and weaknesses of the CRP: (1) findings from the literature, (2) quantitative results from data on recruits entering the Army during the pilot program, and (3) qualitative results from discussions with stakeholders.

Stakeholders reported that the CRP had several strengths or potential strengths, but also some substantial weaknesses. Many (but not all) stakeholders thought that the program had the potential to improve recruiting by offering a broader array of choices to recruits. Reported problems that would need to be addressed in any future test of this type of program included a need for additional, ongoing training and for better information via websites; a need for broad knowledge of opportunities and incentive packages across the Army's components; the ability to use websites to obtain accurate and up-to-date information on opportunities and recruiting processes; incentives and credit for recruiters writing cross-component contracts; and a policy directing how handoffs between components should occur. Additional recommendations to strengthen the program included marketing materials for the other component(s) and broad publicity for successes.

Recruiters' satisfaction with the program was mixed—some said that they saw little value added and even an overall adverse effect on workload, while many at more-successful locations reported that the program helped them make mission and that they regretted its termination. One difference between the sites involved the relationship between the components in the test site pairs: The relationship was better at the more-successful sites. Recruiters there noted several positive aspects of communication and ways to further strengthen it, such as regular meetings of the local recruiters and managers for the components to discuss emerging issues and resolve them.

Broadly, the strengths and weaknesses of the program are consistent with findings in the literature. The potential of the program was acknowledged widely by stakeholders (both recruiters and others within the Army). Nonetheless, despite testing numerous different measures, the research team concluded that the quantitative data consistently indicated that the CRP did not have a statistically meaningful impact on recruiting.

Some outcomes are easier to measure than others; for example, the number of recruits is easier to measure than the recruit-MOS match quality, and some recruiters reported that the broader array of choices was helpful. However, our conversations with recruiters and others in the Army also revealed several problems related to incentives and information. Finally, we have very little information on a broad goal established by the NCFA (2016): the extent to which the CRP served to increase integration across the Army. Given the weak results and mixed perceptions of the pilot program, there is little evidence that the program served to increase Army integration and help the Army operate as a Total Force.

We note here that the weaknesses concerning the implementation of the program are highly likely to have contributed to the absence of meaningful differences in production between the test and comparison sites. While information-related issues and some of the other weaknesses can be addressed, as discussed earlier, a number of these weaknesses are not easily rectified. Importantly, assuring proper credit for recruiting effort in a consolidated environment is not straightforward. According to discussions with recruiters, Army policies, and the research team's past experience with Army recruiting, implementing a solution to provide credit for recruiter effort would require a fundamental change to the Army components' recruiting authorities, operational procedures, and statutes. There are also technical issues involving credit for contracts versus the need to fill training seats and unit vacancies from a given component. Such issues cannot easily be resolved without joint missioning, something that appears unlikely in the near term (or perhaps even the longer term).

Closing Thoughts

While there may be potential for a consolidated recruiting program to improve Army recruiting, the three-year CRP did not appear to result in additional recruits, higher-quality recruits, or increased efficiency. The qualitative results provide an explanation of these findings. In short, members of the recruiting community indicated that they lacked training and other resources necessary to ably explain all options to recruits; additionally, stakeholders had broad agreement that recruiter incentives were not well-aligned and that processes for handing off recruits were not clearly defined. Most of the recommendations provided by stakeholders focused on these areas.

While there were differences between the sites that wrote many cross-component contracts and the other test sites, the sites that wrote many contracts emphasized most of the same challenges as other sites. A key difference is that sites writing many contracts were more likely to state that the program helped them to achieve their recruiting mission.

The three-year pilot program ended during the initial period of the coronavirus disease 2019 (COVID-19) pandemic. The pandemic caused disruption throughout the economy, including within some Army operations. However, there is no evidence that the pandemic drove the results of the CRP; results from the prepandemic period were similar to those that occurred during the brief overlap of the program with the pandemic period.

While our evaluation provided no evidence that the Army's CRP improved recruiting outcomes, it did serve to demonstrate specific challenges that would need to be overcome prior to attempting to launch a successful cross-component recruiting program. In the end, efficiencies through this type of program might be achievable if the motivational and operational impediments discussed above were addressed. At the same time, an increase in the number of recruits enlisted would also depend on the number of youths currently lost due to limitations on writing cross-component contracts and there being training seats and unit vacancies left to fill. In addition, credit for cross-component contracts should not exceed the actual number of same-component contracts written, or training seats and unit vacancies will not be filled. On balance, considering the organizational and operational changes required and related costs, the study team believes it is not likely that the Army can, particularly in the near term, address the challenges that must be overcome to launch a successful cross-component recruiting program.

Discussions with Stakeholders

In this appendix, we provide additional information on the qualitative data that we gathered through conversations with recruiters and with command leadership.

We gathered qualitative data throughout the course of the pilot. We did this using three different methods.

- First, to assess the initial impact of the pilot program, members of the study team visited all pilot site locations. These visits occurred in 2018–2019 (half in each year). There were 13 test site pairs visited that included multiple locations for each of the 13 USAREC Companies and 13 ARNG Teams. At each site, RAND Arroyo researchers conducted semistructured focus groups separately with USAREC or ARNG recruiters.
- We also gathered input from command leadership, both from the Army NGB and from relevant individuals at HQ USAREC. Specifically, the Army NGB provided consolidated feedback for states participating in the pilot program. To gain additional perspective, we interviewed HQ USAREC staff who were directly involved with the management and oversight of the pilot program on October 30, 2020.
- Finally, in late April and early May 2021, we interviewed USAREC and ARNG recruiters at the three test site pair locations that wrote the most cross-component contracts.

In each focus group/interview interaction, we used a similar semistructured protocol to guide our discussion. The protocol is included in the next subsection.

Protocol

1. Overall, based on your experience with the program, how would you assess the Consolidated Recruiting Program and Pilot Test:
   a. Are there positives to highlight? If so, what?
   b. Are there negatives to highlight?
2. Were there ways the program could have been strengthened?
3. Were there obstacles that could not be overcome?
4. What were the major issues/challenges that your command experienced?
   a. Keeping training and internet sites updated?
   b. Issues with getting/giving credit for cross-component enlistments?
   c. Other issues?
5. Overall, based on your experience with the program, does it offer potential benefits to the Army or not?
6. Are there other strengths or weakness that we should be aware of?

There is no protocol associated with the input from the Army NGB because the RAND Arroyo research team did not have the opportunity to speak with the relevant individuals directly. Rather, the Bureau gathered input from the participating states and provided the information to the RAND Arroyo research team directly. As requested, this input includes information about the strengths and the weaknesses of the pilot program.

Below, we include detailed findings from each set of interviews and focus groups.

Detailed Findings from Focus Groups' Discussions

In this section, we provide detailed information from each set of focus groups and discussions.

Recruiter Focus Groups (2018–2019)

To assess the impact of the pilot program, members of the study team visited all pilot site locations, half in 2018 and half in 2019, and conducted semistructured focus groups separately with USAREC and ARNG recruiters at those sites. Most recruiters reported problems concerning the implementation of the pilot program. Much of these involved perceptions of added workload without benefit. Concerns expressed by USAREC and ARNG recruiters focused on the following:

- **Not receiving credit for cross-component contracts** (most USAREC Companies and ARNG recruiters maintained their component-specific contract missions)
- **Limited awareness of the program** (primarily among individuals arriving on station after the initial training for cross-component recruiting had been completed). There was no follow-up training at the time of the focus groups
- **Lack of familiarity with various jobs, enlistment options, or current incentive packages for the other component(s)**, despite the computer tab created for the other component(s) at pilot test sites
- **Lack of familiarity with the steps and paperwork required to process a recruit through the other component, and uncertainty regarding how to describe life in the other component to the potential recruit.**

Many recruiters indicated that if these issues were addressed, they would have a better understanding of the program, which they thought could benefit the Army and potential recruits. Others did not see the value in cross-component recruiting or preferred to hand off potential recruits to recruiters for the other component when they had good working relationships with the other component's recruiters and the potential recruit was not interested in the recruiter's own component(s).

In response to this feedback, USAREC conducted a second round of training at the test sites and updated its online information site provided for recruiters to get the latest information about the program during 2019.

ARNG

The following concerns and challenges were articulated by the pilot ARNG states:

Concerns

- **Both ARNG and USAREC recruiters were challenged to understand and describe the other component** in terms of structure, assignment policy (vacancy-based versus centralized), benefits, bonuses, etc.
- **Training and communication between the components needed to improve, and initial training for cross-component recruiting was insufficient.**
- **Recruiters indicated that this pilot was an interruption to accomplishing their mission.**
- **The return on investment did not seem, to the recruiters, to justify the expenditure of man-hours.**

Additional Program Challenges

- **The ARNG was not confident in USAREC's ability to provide accurate and definitive information regarding ARNG services and benefits** when communicating with and enlisting recruits. **This also holds true for ARNG production recruiters who were providing prospects with information regarding active-component opportunities.**
- **School administrators were often confused regarding whom to call (ARNG or USAREC) for component-specific information.**

The following positive features of the program also were reported.

Positive Aspects

- Of the states that participated in the pilot, almost all reported **improved communication between USAREC Companies and ARNG Teams.**
- The flexibility **to enlist in any component** was the primary benefit of the program.
- From the ARNG perspective, **the program produced additional brand recognition and community awareness of the National Guard thanks to the USAREC force advertising ARNG opportunities.**

HQ USAREC

To obtain additional perspective, we interviewed HQ USAREC staff directly involved in the management and oversight of the pilot program on October 30, 2020. The questions that guided the discussion and a summary of the main points raised are below. In some cases, the answers here are more detailed than those described earlier based on focus groups. This is a function of the different format.

Overall, based on your experience with the program, how would you assess the Consolidated Recruiting Program and Pilot Test? Are there positives to highlight? If so, what?

- **This program opened lines of communication between the ARNG and USAREC at the Company-Team level. The program also opened up options for applicants, helping to avoid losing them.** For example, selling another component makes it possible for a USAR recruiter to provide combat jobs in the ARNG; few such options exist in the USAR.
- **The program led to the establishment of cross-component relationships between USAREC Companies and ARNG Teams that are likely to persist.**
- **USAREC embedded a fusion cell with local ARNG leadership to provide training and to discuss and help to resolve issues.**

Are there negatives to highlight? If so, what?

- **Changes came very quickly after the program started.**
- **The internet site posed some specific problems in providing up-to-date information to all pilot sites.**
- **The level at which organization credit was allocated for cross-component contracts posed a specific issue.** Recruiters initially believed that credit would go all the way through the chain of command; when this changed, resulting in USAR credit only at Company

level, USAREC recruiters had little incentive to enlist soldiers into the ARNG.[1]

- **Too many levels of ARNG and USAREC organizations were involved.** Some units did not take it seriously. There was a lack of leadership in execution; many leaders initially did not buy in.
- **In some cases, recruiters view the other components as competitors; breaking away from this was difficult.**

What were the major issues/challenges that your command experienced? Keeping training and internet sites updated? Issues with getting/giving credit for cross-component enlistments?

- Starting with a **better understanding of recruiters' needs,** and being willing to **make adjustments quickly,** would have strengthened the program. **Publicizing successes broadly** would have been helpful.
- **The major challenges were related to information**: getting initial information very late relative to program start; **not having all information available on a single user-friendly website**; and struggling to standardize when faced with many state-level differences in websites within the ARNG.

Overall, based on your experience with the program, does it offer potential benefits to the Army or not?

In summary, the program does offer potential benefits—given that a small proportion of the U.S. population is qualified to serve and that the capacity to offer additional alternatives within the Army to potential recruits is valuable.

---

[1] From FY 2012, USAREC missioned primarily at the Company level, although increasingly there has been use of individual missions. The situation was further complicated by USAREC not receiving credit for contracts into the RA/USAR written by ARNG recruiters.

Recruiters at Locations with Greater Numbers of Cross-Component Contracts

In late April and early May 2021, we interviewed USAREC and ARNG recruiters at the three test site pairs that wrote the most cross-component contracts. We have consolidated their comments according to their experience with the program. To begin, we note that they reported several problems; many involved the same issues described above. In some instances, they developed effective workarounds.

Negatives

- **There are applicant processing differences between USAREC and the ARNG:** (1) The ARNG can lock an applicant into a job. (2) There are different MEPS procedures. (3) MEPS processing for the ARNG is limited. Stated consequences included the following: (1) Soldiers coming to the ARNG could get the wrong incentive, MOS, etc. (2) Not much knowledge in the ARNG on how to put applicants into the USAR. *Reported remedies included the following: (1) USAREC recruiters used their own MEPS as a workaround once they figured out the ARNG limitation. (2) They should have In Process Reviews with liaisons from each location. More cross-talk would help. (3) More cross-component training at the local level would help.*

- **There was no direct handoff of the recruit.** Stated consequences included the following: Consequence (1): USAREC took a loss on the number of recruits that actually shipped to basic training because of this. RA leads were seen by the ARNG before the RA saw them. They were claimed to be ARNG leads. This created a logistics problem for USAREC: If the ARNG was sending a recruit to the RA, USAREC didn't always know. Recruiters could get a call from the MEPS regarding a package problem. *Reported remedy: In the Active First recruiting program (which required service in the RA prior to the ARNG), the MEPS and Guidance Counselor were ARNG. They handled processing into the RA. This worked well.* Consequence (2): The ARNG lost recruits because USAREC handled ARNG recruits. Originally, the ARNG recruiter didn't meet the applicant until ship day. There was not enough cross-talk at the operations level, which resulted in information needed by or useful to the recruit or recruiter being missing.

Delays cause applicants to lose faith. *Reported remedy: Recruiters had to develop an introduction program.* Consequence (3): The ARNG had training pipeline losses for USAREC recruits into the ARNG because of a lack of communication. USAREC recruiters would lose sight of the applicant, who would fall over to the ARNG. ARNG recruiters are responsible for getting USAREC recruits into ARNG units and through the training pipeline. They drill with recruits one weekend per month for that purpose. *Reported remedy: Recruiters should physically hand off recruits.*

- **On the ARNG side, the internet links could have been better:** Stated consequences included the following: (1) USAREC recruiters did not have full information on the ARNG. (2) Internet information was outdated and problematic. The tab showing details for the other component was outdated. (3) ARNG system vacancies were not fully visible. *Reported remedies: (1) Liaisons at the MEPS helped. (2) An ARNG Team had a spreadsheet with all the vacancies by unit in its state. They wanted the same for the USAR units and needed unit points of contact.*

- **The website was not good enough for the RA.** Stated consequences included the following: Consequence (1): A lot of the USAREC website was not available to ARNG recruiters. *Reported remedies: (1) The ARNG worked issues through communication with the USAREC first sergeant. (2) USAREC should have put the ARNG on USAREC's distribution list for recruiting and program information.* Consequence (2): ZIP Codes outside the ARNG Team's footprint did not always work in the USAREC system; the problem could emerge at the MEPS. *Reported remedy: USAREC overcame this after a couple of instances.*

- **Training was needed for later recruiter arrivals after initial training:** Stated consequences included the following: (1) Recruiters got the initial training, but there were many changes after they were trained. There was no continuous training. (2) Recruiters had three to four ARNG Team leadership changes. (3) Recruiters' training on the program was before the current USAREC Commanding Officer arrived. The new USAREC section chief was not familiar with the program. New arrivals needed to be told about the program by the other recruiters. The rotation every two to three years hurts. (4) Recruiters did not get training on how to view available jobs. Information came from the first sergeant. *Reported remedies: (1) Recruiters needed bi-weekly/ monthly/quarterly training on the process. (2) Recruiters also need training meetings with the leadership on problems and approaches to fix them.*

- **The RA mission was high in number.** Reported consequences included the following: (1) The contracts that the ARNG wrote took away from contracts that could potentially have been written by USAREC. USAREC recruiters got no RA credit but lost this supply of potential recruits. The RA mission did not come down in response to ARNG contracts into RA. (2) Some ARNG recruiters rotated and took contracts with them. *Reported remedy: If RA/USAR recruiters received credit for contracts written into the RA or USAR by the ARNG, that would help generate recruiter support for consolidated recruiting.*

- **ARNG recruiters got credit for RA contracts but got credit for recruits into the ARNG only at state level.** Stated consequences included the following: (1) Credit was not considered adequately. Recruiters were not sure where non-shippers were accounted for. (2) The ARNG Teams had a target of 11 percent market share, but USAREC got the credit for contracts into the ARNG. (3) The totals did not tell where the market share came from. The program reduced ARNG recruiters' chance to get a bonus for producing over mission contracts. Note: The credit policy was not universal; some recruiters got credit for all cross-component contracts. *Reported remedies: (1) Credit would even the playing field. The Army would get more contracts (incentive to write them). For most places, this means Company (USAREC) versus individual recruiter missioning and credit (ARNG). For the ARNG, there was individual missioning, but the state got credit, not individual recruiters. (2) The market share distinction would help.*

The recruiters also reported several positive program features.

Positives

- **The program allowed a one-stop shop:** It was easier for potential recruits to get a full perspective. Potential recruits don't know about the differences between components. This program gives recruiters the ability to explain all of what the Army has to offer. This better serves the applicant by providing a full picture and all opportunities.

- **The program provides additional opportunities for applicants:** (1) For example, for qualification issues, half of the waivers sent to the ARNG that would have been a problem for USAREC were approved. (2) AFQT Category IV vacancies in the ARNG also were available. (3) Exceptions to policy such as overfill of local reserve units also were easier. (4) It was faster to get waivers and overfill in the ARNG. (5) The ARNG also had combat jobs. (6) The RA option allowed an applicant working with an ARNG recruiter to join the RA to get a full-time job or get out of a dangerous area. (7) The program gave the applicant the ability to switch over in the middle of the process without the applicant or recruiter losing the work done. (8) Training was more available in the ARNG. The soldier aspect also was better in the ARNG there versus the USAR (i.e., there were more training resources and shorter training turnaround times).

- **Recruiters took advantage of the program to help make mission.** Many reported that it was a big help. (1) USAREC to ARNG contracts counted toward the USAR mission. For example, they were able to recruit prospects interested in combat arms who wanted to remain in the area. They were successful in meeting mission over the test period, partly due to the program. (2) The program expanded the RA market. This USAREC Company got a good portion of RA recruits from coordination. Fewer documents were needed for RA contracts.

  USAREC lost some of this now that the program was ended. They did not lose contracts to the ARNG. (3) Recruiters at one particular site got credit at the Company level for both cross-component directions. The ARNG got credit for USAREC contracts, though most often at the state level. (4) The program helped both components to meet end strength. (5) It made life easier working together. Having two Army representatives at local high school career days when competing with other services also was a plus. If recruiters needed an asset (e.g., a rock wall for a high school visit) they could coordinate with the ARNG and split credit for recruits. USAREC could capitalize on ARNG recruiters' longevity and local networks. USAREC recruiters became more interactive with colleges. (6) The National Guard MEPS were open during COVID; USAREC's were not. One USAREC Company was able to leverage this.

- **Some USAREC recruiters had many contacts with the ARNG. There was a lot of coordination. This built rapport, including with applicants.** (1) ARNG recruiters communicated more with the MEPS when not with the local USAREC Company. On the field side, they had good relationships with other recruiters. (2) Recruiters from the reporting USAREC Company worked with a master sergeant from the ARNG. They talked at least once every two weeks. It was seamless with the local ARNG Team on vacancies. They also had the drop-down menu in the recruiter site for the ARNG. (3) For the reporting ARNG recruiters the handoffs worked pretty well. The handoffs were in house, and one person was used for them. The recruiters found this to be helpful. Battalion Operations would get a recruit to the ARNG during COVID.

Abbreviations

AFQT	Armed Forces Qualification Test
AIT	Advanced Individual Training
ARNG	Army National Guard
ASA (M&RA)	Assistant Secretary of the Army (Manpower and Reserve Affairs)
CA	combat arms
CRP	Consolidated Recruiting Program
CS	combat support
CSS	combat service support
DEP	Delayed Entry Program
FY	fiscal year
HQ	headquarters
HQDA (G-1)	Headquarters Department of the Army, G-1
IPT	Integrated Process Team
MEPS	Military Entrance Processing Station
MOS	Military Occupational Specialty
NCFA	National Commission on the Future of the Army
NDAA	National Defense Authorization Act
NGB	National Guard Bureau
OPT	Operational Planning Team
OSUT	One Station Unit Training
RA	Regular Army
RC	reserve components
RSID	Recruiting Station Identification Code
USAR	U.S. Army Reserve
USAREC	U.S. Army Recruiting Command

Bibliography

Arkes, Jeremy, and Jesse M. Cunha, "Workplace Goals and Output Quality: Evidence from Time-Constrained Recruiting Goals in the US Navy," *Defence and Peace Economics*, Vol. 26, No. 5, 2015, pp. 491–515.

Arkes, Jeremy, and M. Rebecca Kilburn, *Modeling Reserve Recruiting: Estimates of Enlistments*, Santa Monica, Calif.: RAND Corporation, MG-202-OSD, 2005. As of February 22, 2022:
https://www.rand.org/pubs/monographs/MG202.html

Asch, Beth J., *Reserve Supply in the Post Desert Storm Recruiting Environment*, Santa Monica, Calif.: RAND Corporation, MR-224, 1993. As of February 22, 2022:
https://www.rand.org/pubs/monograph_reports/MR224.html

Asch, Beth J., *Navigating Current and Emerging Army Recruiting Challenges: What Can Research Tell Us?* Santa Monica, Calif.: RAND Corporation, RR-3107-A, 2019. As of February 22, 2022:
https://www.rand.org/pubs/research_reports/RR3107.html

Asch, Beth J., and Paul Heaton, *An Analysis of the Incidence of Recruiter Irregularities*, Santa Monica, Calif.: RAND Corporation, TR-827-OSD, 2010. As of February 22, 2022:
https://www.rand.org/pubs/technical_reports/TR827.html

Buddin, Richard, and Carole Roan Gresenz, *Assessment of Combined Active/ Reserve Recruiting Programs*, Santa Monica, Calif.: RAND Corporation, MR-504-A, 1994. As of March 30, 2022:
https://www.rand.org/pubs/monograph_reports/MR504.html

Dertouzos, James N., and Steven Garber, *Human Resource Management and Army Recruiting: Analyses of Policy Options*, Santa Monica, Calif.: RAND Corporation, MG-433-A, 2006. As of February 22, 2022:
https://www.rand.org/pubs/monographs/MG433.html

Desrosiers, Shannon, Josh Horvath, and Jared Huff with Chris Gonzales, *Evaluating the Services' Recruiting Policies: Recruiter Management, Missioning, Incentives, and Selection*, Arlington, Va.: CNA, 2019.

Dynarski, Susan, C. J. Libassi, Katherine Michelmore, and Stephanie Owen, "Closing the Gap: The Effect of a Targeted, Tuition-Free Promise on College Choices of High-Achieving, Low-Income Students," National Bureau of Economic Research Working Paper 25349, December 2018.

Headquarters Department of the Army, *Consolidation of Army Marketing and Pilot Program on Consolidated Army Recruiting: Report to Congress*, Arlington, Va., June 2018.

Headquarters Department of the Army, *Consolidation of Army Marketing and Pilot Program on Consolidated Army Recruiting: Report to Congress*, Arlington, Va., June 2019.

Knapp, David, Bruce R.Orvis, Christopher E. Maerzluft, and Tiffany Berglund, *Resources Required to Meet the U.S. Army's Enlisted Recruiting Requirements Under Alternative Recruiting Goals, Conditions, and Eligibility Policies*, Santa Monica, Calif.: RR-2364-A, 2018. As of February 22, 2022: https://www.rand.org/pubs/research_reports/RR2364.html

National Commission on the Future of the Army, *Report to the President and Congress of the United States*, Washington, D.C., January 28, 2016.

NCFA—*See* National Commission on the Future of the Army.

Oken, Carole, and Beth J. Asch, *Encouraging Recruiter Achievement: A Recent History of Military Recruiter Incentive Programs*, Santa Monica, Calif.: RAND Corporation, MR-845-OSD/A, 1997. As of August 29, 2021: https://www.rand.org/pubs/monograph_reports/MR845.html

Orvis, Bruce R., Craig A. Bond, Daniel Schwam, and Irineo Cabreros, *Resources Required to Meet U.S. Army Reserve's Enlisted Recruiting Requirements Under Alternative Recruiting Goals, Conditions, and Eligibility Policies*, Santa Monica, Calif.: RAND Corporation, RR-A1304-1, forthcoming.

Orvis, Bruce R., Christopher E. Maerzluft, Sung-Bou Kim, Michael G. Shanley, and Heather Krull, *Prospective Outcome Assessment for Alternative Recruit Selection Policies*, Santa Monica, Calif.: RR-2267-A, 2018. As of February 22, 2022: https://www.rand.org/pubs/research_reports/RR2267.html

Polich, J. Michael, James N. Dertouzos, and S. James Press, *The Enlistment Bonus Experiment*, Santa Monica, Calif.: RAND Corporation, R-3353-FMP, 1986. As of February 22, 2022: https://www.rand.org/pubs/reports/R3353.html

Polich, J. Michael, Richard L. Fernandez, and Bruce R. Orvis, *Enlistment Effects of Military Educational Benefits*, Santa Monica, Calif.: RAND Corporation, N-1783-MRAL, 1982. As of February 22, 2022: https://www.rand.org/pubs/notes/N1783.html

Public Law 114-328, National Defense Authorization Act for Fiscal Year 2017, December 23, 2016.

Simon, Curtis J., Sebastian Negrusa, and John T. Warner, "Educational Benefits and Military Service: An Analysis of Enlistment, Reenlistment, and Veterans' Benefit Usage 1991–2005," *Economic Inquiry*, Vol. 48, No. 4, 2010, pp. 1008–1031.

Tan, Hong W., *Non-Prior Service Reserve Enlistments: Supply Estimates and Forecasts*, Santa Monica, Calif.: RAND Corporation, R-3786-FMP/RA, 1991. As of April 11, 2022:
https://www.rand.org/pubs/reports/R3786.html

Warner, John T., Curtis J. Simon, and Deborah M. Payne, *Enlistment Supply in the 1990's: A Study of the Navy College Fund and Other Enlistment Incentive Programs*, Seaside, Calif.: Defense Manpower Data Center Report No. 2000–015, 2001.

Wenger, Jennie W., Trey Miller, Matthew D. Baird, Peter Buryk, Lindsay Daugherty, Marlon Graf, Simon Hollands, Salar Jahedi, and Douglas Yeung, *Are Current Military Education Benefits Efficient and Effective for the Services?* Santa Monica, Calif.: RAND Corporation, RR-1766-OSD, 2017. As of February 22, 2022:
https://www.rand.org/pubs/research_reports/RR1766.html